THE
LOST LANGUAGE
OF THE STARS

Virevolte

Star Symbol Stone

From early childhood, I have delighted in watching the stars; enchanted by the patterns of lights they formed. On clear dark nights I would spend hours, wrapped in layers of jumpers and scarves, looking up at the sky, drawn by the beauty and the sense of immense distance and time. Although I lived on the north-west edge of Dundee, with the competing glare of the city street-lights, I could make out the familiar constellations; the Plough, the great belted figure of Orion, the W of Cassiopia. These were the designs that I first read about in books for amateur astronomers. On occasions when I was able to visit the countryside, away from the city lights, I could attempt to pick out the outlines of other constellations, including the zodiac figures familiar from the horoscope pages of magazines. As I gradually learned to recognise these constellations in the sky, I learned from avid reading that most of the star signs that we know today originated in ancient times; in Babylon, Egypt and Assyria. The brightest stars bore beautiful enigmatic arabic names. Characters from the Greek myths were among the imagined figures marching across our night skies.

I lived quite near to the farmlands stretching from the city edges towards the Sidlaws, the fairy hills. Walking out past fields of tatties, barley and kale I came across the carved stones of the Picts for the first time in the shape of Martin's Stone, in a field of South Balluderon farm near Tealing. At that time I had no idea who had made these images. They were connected to local tales of saintly youths rescuing maidens from greedy dragons. Later on, I found more of these stones in the Dundee Museum and learnt a little more about their history, about the people who had lived in the underground houses called by the french name souter-rains, and who had built massive hill-forts at the entrances to the Angus glens. I wanted to know more about these people who were, after all, family; a fair number of generations removed perhaps, but nevertheless I felt an attachment to them. I discovered that these people were called Picts; not their own name but a given name first mentioned in the writings of Eumenius the Roman; and that they themselves had left no writings. Histories of the Picts were based on observations made by foreigners, not always reliable, always coloured by the opinions of the observer. Their origins were hotly disputed by historians; their spoken language had been forgotten. In place of words the Picts left a legacy of wonderful carved designs; eloquent statements in stone about their concepts and beliefs. With the formation of the kingdom of Alba under Cináed mac Ailpín around 843, the Picts seemed to disappear from history; indeed the Declaration of Arbroath signed in 1320 specifically claimed that the Picts had been completely eliminated, 'Pictis omnino deletis'. It seemed likely however, that although the ruling elite may have changed, the majority of the people who had once been called Picts carried on living, farming, having families, making up a large proportion of the population of the country which was later to be given the name Scotland.

It was to be some years later before these two interests of astronomy and history would combine in a wholly unexpected way. A late Autumn evening, cold and clear; the ground made hard as stone with frost. As I stood looking up at the sky, following the curving lines of stars, I noticed something astonishing. I could make out the shape of the strange beastie carved on the Pictish stones; first the head and then the line of its back and the curls of its limbs. During the coming weeks I realised that other symbols could be picked out among the stars. I began to think of a time when people in the north of what is now Scotland looked up at the skies without the knowledge of the system of constellations that we have been taught. Direct observation of the night sky and direct experience of the natural world combined in the formation of images. 2000 or so years ago the stars were the inspiration for designs still visible today on the sacred stones of the people known as Picts; spiralling clusters of stars interpreted as the flowing spirals in skillfully worked designs of animals, birds and geometric shapes.

In the following illustrations I have chosen examples of the designs, symbolic images found on the earliest, pre-christian stones, and these are presented as line drawings. I have added simplified diagrams which can be used in conjunction with conventional star charts as an aid to locating the symbols among the stars. I have indicated the positions in the sky of the asterisms with reference to one or two guiding stars. The diagrams show the brighter stars in the pictish constellations, joined to give an idea of the imaginary lines formed in the mind. As well as these chains of bright stars, less intense stars add to the sense of image when they form lines and spirals; or when they cluster together to provide a glowing area of sky in contrast with very dark starless areas of sky; so that much more subtle images of light and shade are observed than can be demonstrated in the diagrams.

There are symbols in the north on view every clear night throughout the year; guiding stars for navigators. Then there are the seasonal groups of the south; rising and falling as pointers of the year. Low in the sky skimming the southern horizon the animals, stag, wolf, bear, boar and horse, slowly mark time. Between the horse of summer and the winter stag, around the time of the autumn equinox; the bright blue-white star Fomalhaut can be glimpst very low on the horizon amidst a dusting of faint stars, in the deep-dark void of one of the most barren areas of the sky, just below the shimmering silver salmon.

The stones chosen by the Picts for their monuments are local. Some may have been standing stones long before they were adorned with symbols. Many are slabs of grey, pink or red sandstone. Some are heavy, dark whinstone. Others are fine pieces of the hard stones, gneiss, granite and gabbro.

In addition to the numerous carved stones of the Picts and a few metal objects which have survived the centuries of violence and destruction, examples of the symbols have survived on the walls of east coast sea caves. In Fife, a group of villages are named the Wemyss, meaning the place of caves. At East Weymss 8000-years-old raised sea-caves above the silvery mica-sand beach have been used for a variety of purposes since the bronze age. A number of designs which seem to be early forms of the symbols are carved on the sandstone walls. These may hold clues to the development from the simple connecting lines imagined by the star watchers, to the refined images; some rich with elaborate knotwork, others elegantly plain.

For each symbol illustrated, I have included a brief discussion of its essential meaning. In these discussions I have included comparisons with other ancient belief systems in order to explore similarities in form and meaning. I have referred to close neighbours of the historical Picts and also to peoples far away in distance and time. The Picts were a trading people, and the busy sea-routes carried not only goods to be exchanged, but a sharing of ideas, a telling of stories, news and fresh discoveries from remote lands. Knowledge of the symbolism used by other cultures, and an exploration of the traces of meaning which survived into historical eras, can provide us with clues about the meanings held within the symbols of the Picts.

WINTER STARS

fig. 1   **The Star Beastie on grey sandstone at Brodie**

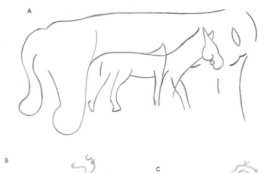

fig. 3   Star beasties from the caves at East Weymss.
A, B and C are from Jonathon's Cave. A is faintly marked, above and partly overlapping the design of a horse.
B and C were destroyed by arsonists in 1986.
D and E are from Court Cave and F was in the West Doo Cave which collapsed during the first world war. Drawings are not to scale.

10

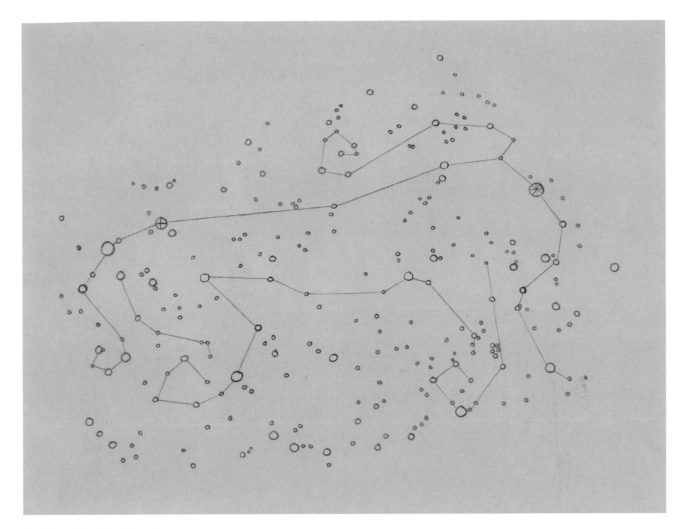

fig. 2 **The Star Beastie**
guiding stars: Capella (Alpha Aurigae) and Castor (Alpha Geminorum)

The great star beastie is the largest of all the star groups. While other zoomorphic symbols are clear and very vital representations of recognisable native birds and animals; this wonderful beast - unique to the Picts - is unfamiliar and strange to us. Its fluid, flowing lines speak of a watery nature; its graceful head is gentle. On the Brodie stone, found in 1781, the beastie is decorated with the knotwork that speaks to us of the interconnectedness of life and of the artist's delight in the intricacies of geometry. At the Autumn equinox the star beastie rises in the east and sets in the west. One of the brightest stars in the sky - Capella - is set in its forehead.

fig. 4   **The Wolf on red granite from Newbiggen**

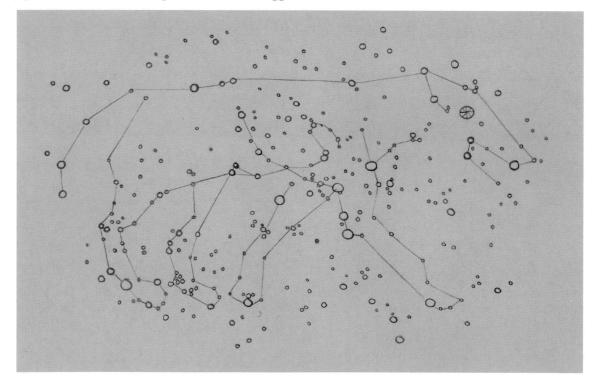

fig. 5   **The Wolf**
guiding star: Sirius (Alpha Canis Majoris)

The grey wolf - canis lupus - howls at the moon, comes close in winter, takes the sick and the old from the herds. In this role he is the bringer of death. His stars are the dead of winter stars. However, the wolf befriended becomes the guardian dog; protector of the herds and hearth, companion on long treks through heather and gorse. In the Orkneys a neolithic tomb at Cuween contained the skulls of dogs. Sirius we know as the dog star, rising around the end of October and setting around the end of February. In Greek it is Seirios, the scorching star. Various peoples saw in the wolf the victory of darkness over light. In the Balkan countries there is a story that eclipses of the sun and moon are caused by dog-headed monsters. In Celtic mythology a wolf swallows the sky father - the sun - each night; while the wolf was the Scandinavian great winter who swallows the sun. The wolf was one of the symbols of Woden in his role as guide to the underworld.

fig. 6   **The Double Disc on sandstone from Dunnichen**

Formed from two of the brightest stars in the winter sky, the double disc is representative of duality. It may depict the thunderbolt with its connotations of great power and strength. Certain forms of cup and ring mark, carved at least as far back as the bronze age, show an affinity with this symbol, notably on the Clach-na-Cruich at Fernan. Symbols remarkably like the double-disc with Z-branch, and the crescent with V-branch, have been found in the Marne valley area of France, while double-discs known as eye symbols have been found in megalithic graves as far apart as Denmark and the Western Mediteranean. There are double discs on an axe-shaped stone found in the graveyard at Sanda in Gotland. A similar form is found in the the Tibetan Dorje symbol.

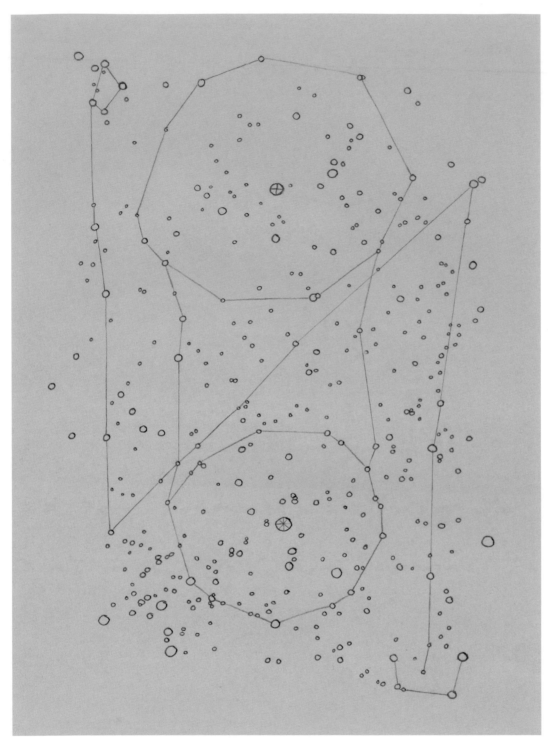

fig. 7   **The Double Disc**
guiding stars: Sirius (Alpha Canis Majoris) and Procyon (Alpha Canis Minoris)

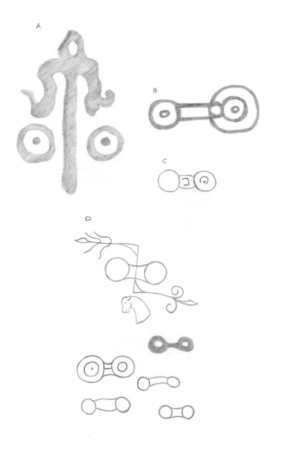

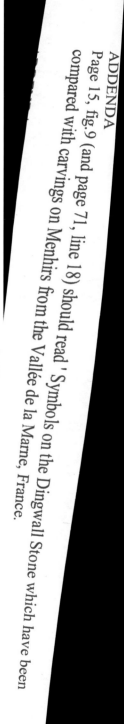

ADDENDA

Page 15, fig.9 (and page 71, line 18) should read ' Symbols on the Dingwall Stone which have been compared with carvings on Menhirs from the Vallée de la Marne, France.

fig. 8   Double discs from the walls of the East Weymss caves.
A and B are from Court Cave.
C is from Sloping Cave, and D, a selection of double disc designs, including a very fine example with floriated Z-branch and an animal head, were lost in the collapsed ruins of the West Doo Cave.
Drawings are not to scale.

fig. 9   Menhirs from the Vallée de la Marne, France.

fig. 10   **The Winter Giant on sandstone from Golspie**

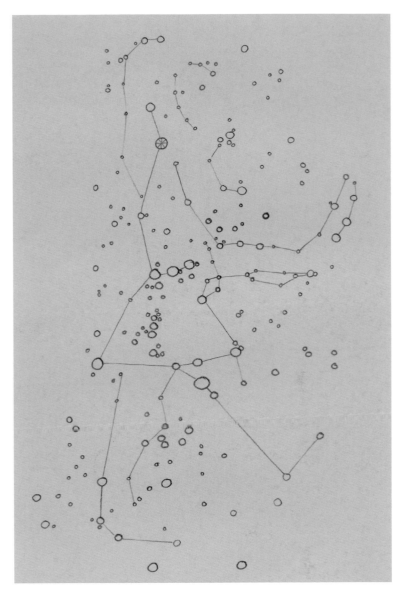

fig. 11　**The Winter Giant**
guiding star: Betelgeuse (Alpha Orionis)

One of the giant-men of the North. Resonant of the great sky giants Orion/Osiris. In Hibernia he was An Selgaire Mhór, the Great Hunter. We do not know what the Picts called him. These men come from the shadows of the past. They carry the ancient weapons of axe and dagger, not the later swords and spears. The man from Golspie holds a weapon which might be the jaw-bone of an animal. We can imagine his presence, lurking in the mists among the high creagan. He is the winter giant of the Picts, succeeded in the summer months by the giant depicted at Rhynie.

fig. 12   Two designs of giants, with double discs perhaps representing thunderbolts, from the East Weymss Caves.
A is from Jonathon's Cave. B is from Court Cave.
Drawings are not to scale.

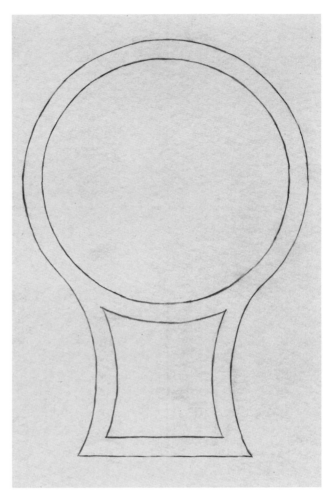

fig. 13   **The Well on sandstone at Meigle**

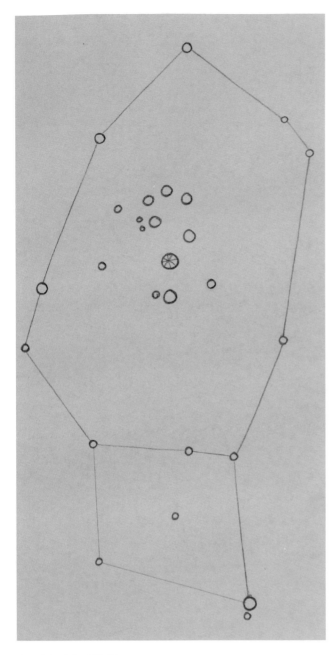

fig. 14   **The Well**
guiding star: Alcyone (Eta Tauri)

This is the well of stars. At Burghead fort there is a very large and impressive well. Twenty steps lead down into the darkness where there is a large square chamber cut from the solid rock. Within this chamber is a stone tank. Although in reality this is quite shallow, in the darkness of the chamber the water appears black and deep. In this land of rain and wet mist, harvests to be gathered in the face of approaching storms and never far from the wild northern seas; water was granted respect. Wells, places with watery womb-like qualities, were associated with female spirits or deities. These special places were often given a Christian identity and are still named after saints. At one time over six hundred holy wells could be counted within Scotland. F Marian McNeill gives some interesting accounts of rituals connected with these wells in her collection of folklore and festival, The Silver Bough. Significant too are the healing waters trapped in boulders such as those near Loch Tay; the slate stone Clach-na-Cruich at Fernan; and Fuaran na Druidh Chasad, a large quartz-veined mica schist, at Killin. Water from these stones was still being used to treat illnesses until the middle of the nineteenth century. In Celtic mythology the sacred wells gave access to the other world, and contained waters with healing or magical properties.

fig. 15   **Stars on grey sandstone at Brodie**

A clear depiction of a spiral group of stars, the star group we know as the Pliedes, protected between the bodies of two twinned watery beings. Under normal conditions six stars can be seen clearly in the Pliedes, the seventh seeming to appear and disappear due to its variable nature. There were reputedly seven ancient kingdoms of the Picts; each kingdom a pair. These were: Enegus cum Moerne, Adtheodle et Gouerin, Stradeern cum Meneted, Fif cum Fothreue, Marr cum Buchen, Muref et Ross and Cathanesia citra montem et ultra montem. When the sky is exceptionally clear, nine bright stars can be observed. There are many traditions of local goddesses, female protective spirits and groups of maidens from three to nine in number linked with wells, springs, rocks and mounds in the old land of the Picts. Complex systems of number symbolism were used by Celts, Teutons and the early Scandinavians; this group was known by Germanic people as the seven sisters. In Norse myth the god Heimdall, guardian of the bridge leading to Asgard, was the offspring of nine giant maidens connected to the sea. The importance of this cluster of stars can be traced back to some of the oldest pictorial representations in the world. In the Grotte de Lascaux, six dots painted above the head of an auroch has been recognised as a depiction of the star group, which is thought to have been a marker of the spring and autumn equinox.

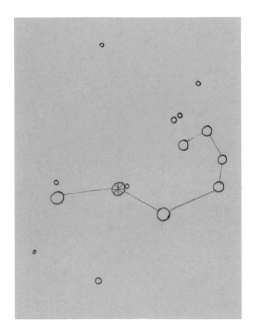

fig. 16 **The Stars in the Well**
guiding star: Alcyone (Eta Tauri)

fig. 17 Auroch with Pliedes, from a palaeolithic painting, in oches and lamp black, in the Grotte de Lascaux, Dordogne, France.

fig. 18 **The Bull on white sandstone from Burghead**

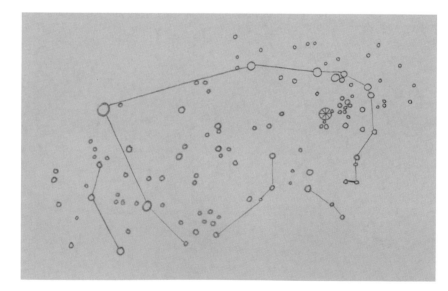

fig. 19 **The Bull**
guiding star Aldebaran
(Alpha Tauri)

A symbol of strength and virility in many cultures, the bull stones have been found only at Burghead, a large timber-laced fort situated at the centre of northern Pictland. The fort had particularly fine bulls incised on its walls. They may have been carved prior to the building of the fort and then reused. Unfortunately, the great stones on which they were carved were used to build a harbour in the 19th century and only six stones have yet been rediscovered; thirty are recorded in old records. It is possible that at Burghead, the bull - of great importance to Celtic beliefs - had overshadowed the older star animal. From the Scottish Gaelic tradition we have this description of a monsterous bull. By the light of the moon the targh uisge rises from the waves, its great head black as a thunder cloud, its nostrils fiery red, bringing terror to the land. Targh uisge means literally water bull, and the similarity in sound to the zodiac Taurus is remarkable. The Babylonians saw their great bull of the heavens, Gu-an-na, as being in the bright star cluster the hyades.

fig. 20 **The Red Deer on sandstone from Ardross**

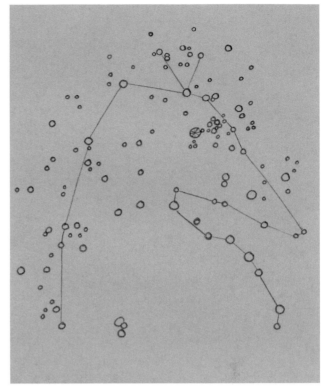

fig. 21 **The Red Deer**
guiding star: Aldebaran (Alpha Tauri)

This elegant animal is a sensitive portrait of a native red deer; a young male with new velvet-covered antlers. Here is an alternative interpretation of the stars seen by people deep in antiquity as the head of a bull.

fig. 22 **The Stag on schist from Grantown**

Cervus elaphus scoticus is the red deer; survivor of the ice-age, roaring in the great caledonian forests. The stag's antlers are seen as symbolising the tree of life, representing creation and hence sexual union. Where we can read the antlers of the stag, the Babylonians saw a great branch rising before the bull. In Celtic mythology deer were divine messengers from the other-world, herded by the fairies. The Celts wore deer skin and antlers in sacred rituals and believed that their goddess, Flidass of the wild things, rode in a chariot drawn by deer. In Tibetan Bon ceremonies the antlered deer is a prominent figure in the masked dramas depicting the struggle between good and evil.

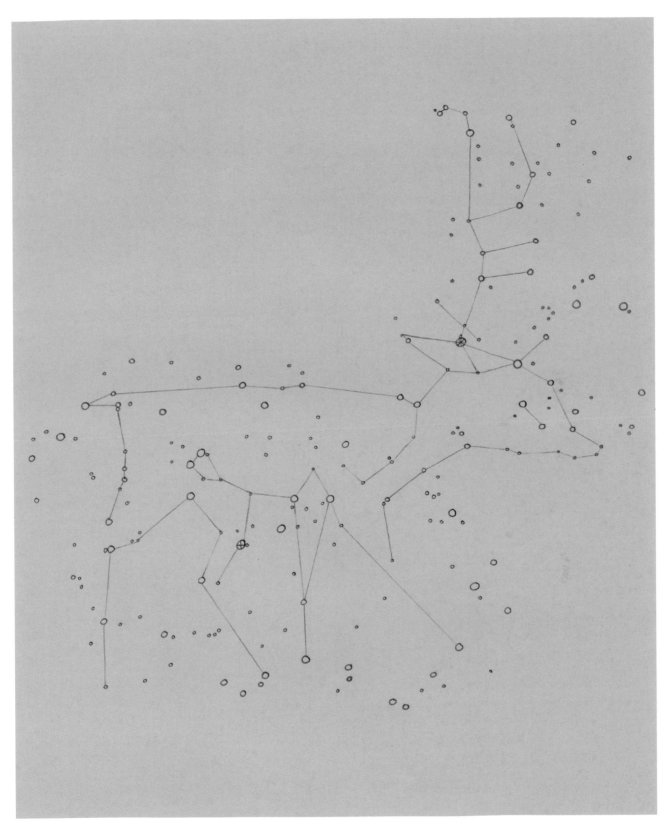

fig. 23   **The Stag**
guiding stars: Menkar (Alpha Ceta) and Zaurak (Gamma Eridani)

SPRING STARS

fig. 24   **The Goose on sandstone from Easterton of Roseisle**

This plump, healthy bird, the greylag goose anser anser, was discovered in 1895 on a stone built into a burial cist. She checks behind, ever watchful, a vigilant guard goose ready to give a loud warning of intruders. The migration of geese in great noisy flights are important markers of the seasons. Their numbers increase as wintering flocks arrive. In Spring the geese are moving north in arrow formations, flying off to Iceland and the northern coasts for summer. A Celtic symbol of war and an attribute of war gods. The Nile goose, the great chatterer, is the creator of the world in ancient Egyptian mythology; an emblem too, of Isis, Osiris and Horus. This star group would have looked slightly different to the Pictish starwatchers. The star Arcturus, marking the goose's tail, is an exceptionally quick-moving star and has travelled, in relation to the other goose stars, a distance roughly equivalent to twice the moon's diameter over the last two thousand years.

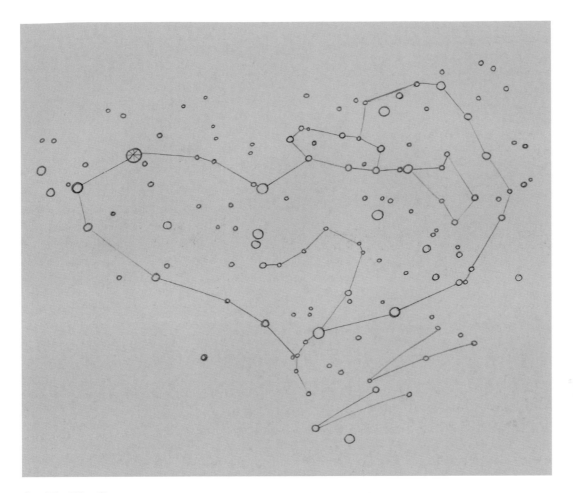

fig. 25   **The Goose**
   guiding star: Arcturus (Alpha Boötes)

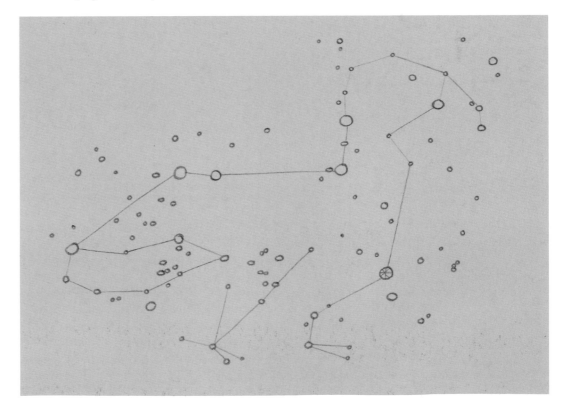

fig. 27   **The Eagle**
   guiding star: Regulus (Alpha Leonis)

fig. 26　**The Eagle on blue gneiss at Strathpeffer**

In 1918 a lonely white sea-eagle was shot from the skies above the Orkneys. She was the last of the native sea-eagles, haliacetus albicilla, in Gaelic Iolaire-suile-na-grein, the eagle with the sunlit eye.

The eagle sees far and clear. Great intelligence is attributed to her. In the Orkneys there is evidence, from around 3000BCE, of the practise of exposing bodies to the elements before burial of the remains. This is most notable in the Tomb of the Eagles at Isbister on South Ronaldsay which contained the bones of both humans and great sea eagles. The human remains were mainly skulls with few arm or leg bones, showing clearly that bones and not whole bodies were buried. Smaller bones more easily carried off by the eagles or wild animals were missing. During the 1970's a few pairs were re-introduced to Scotland from Norway, and these awe-inspiring birds, with wing spans of over eight feet, soar again over the sea-cliffs of the west coast. In the Eryri mountains of the Cymry white eagles were seen as oracles of peace and war. In Scandinavian lore, depicted on carved stone, the eagle of light battles against the serpent of darkness in the branches of the yggdasil tree of life. In ancient Egypt this constellation was a lion, while the Babylonians saw it as a dog.

fig. 28   **The Bear on sandstone from Old Scatness Broch**

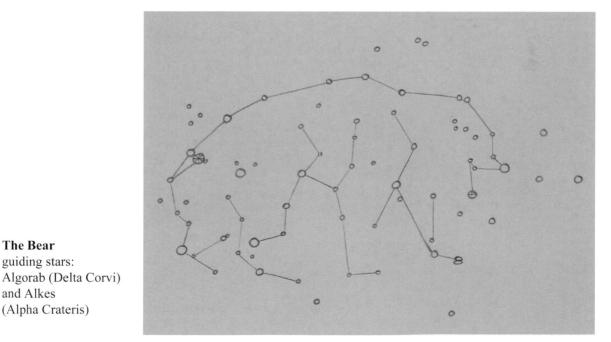

fig. 29   **The Bear**
guiding stars:
Algorab (Delta Corvi)
and Alkes
(Alpha Crateris)

The symbol of the bear has been recently rediscovered on a slab found in the Shetlands in 2003. The hibernating bear is the animal of resurrection and birth. The brown bear, ursa arctos, was one of the native animals found in the land of the Picts. Many were removed by the Romans, shipped out to die fighting in the arenas. On the stones which have survived the ages; the most numerous designs are the crescents of which ninety-four are known, eighty of the double-disc and forty-nine of the star animal. There are twenty-four known serpents, but animals as symbols, as distinct from the numerous animals forming part of the story scenes on later stones, are relatively sparse. At present, three wolves, three geese, three deer, three boar, one horse and now one bear, have been found.

SUMMER STARS

fig. 30   **The Summer Giant on gabbro from Rhynie**

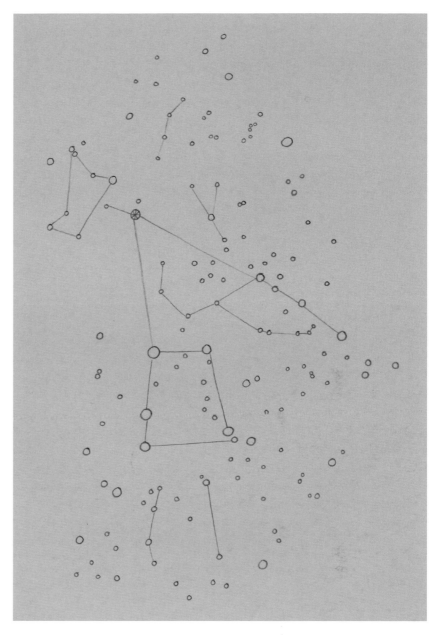

fig. 31　**The Summer Giant**
guiding star: Ras Algetha (Alpha Herculis)

Here is the axe-man of the Picts, from a stone found at Rhynie in Strathbogie. Nearby is Tap o' Noth, the remains of a rectangular hill fort at a height of 1800 feet. It covered around 50 acres and sheltered a community of Picts in 200 timber round houses. Turn to face the pole star in the north, and then lift your eyes to find this giant with his axe raised overhead. Beautiful stone axes have been found which date from early neolithic times. Some are highly polished, showing no signs of having ever been used as tools or in anger. In a hazel wood, at Creag na Caillich by Loch Tay, axes were fashioned from fine grey-green hornfel. Around 1901, at nearby Balnahannait, a small axe sparkling with mica was found, its surfaces decorated with interlaced knotwork. Later, metal axes were fashioned; first from bronze and then from iron. The thunder god Donar, rumbling above the great oak forests of northern Europe has been identified with Gilgamesh, with the Roman Jupiter and with Hercules. His symbol was the axe, standing for the power of lightening. The axe has important symbolic meaning, and is used as a ritual tool in many ancient traditions. The stars of Rhynie man can also be seen as the ancient swaztika symbol of the cosmos.

fig. 32   Four men, on a sandstone, form a swaztika. This is from a
recumbent gravestone, stone number 9, at Meigle.

fig. 33 **The Crescent on red sandstone from Hilton of Cadboll**

Most clearly seen during summer when it is high in the sky, the crescent can be observed during most of the year, appearing low on the horizon in March. The crescent is rich in symbolic meaning. As crescent moon it represents the great mother; while, observed during a solar eclipse, it is a powerful symbol of death and rebirth. A crescent can also be seen to describe a pair of horns and is thus linked to the fertility and masculinity symbolism widely given to horns and horned animals. Yet another crescent shape can be observed as the sun rises or sets on the horizen. The Eagle tomb at Isbister is in the shape of a crescent. The Druids retained the crescent as one of their main symbols.

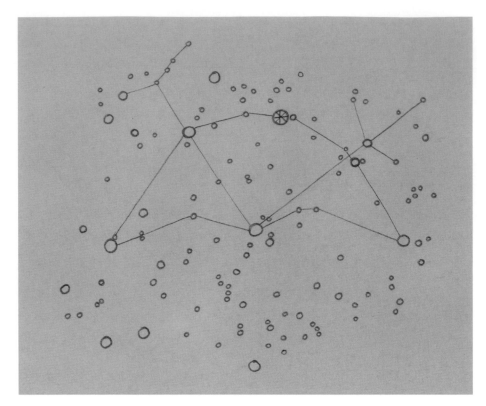

fig. 34 **The Crescent**
guiding star: Deneb (Alpha Cygni)

fig. 35 Isbister Chambered Cairn, the Tomb of the Eagles, on a slope above the cliffs on South Ronaldsay, in the Orkneys. The entrance to the burial chambers faces the sea to the south-west.

fig. 36   **The Mirror and Comb on sandstone from Dunnichen**

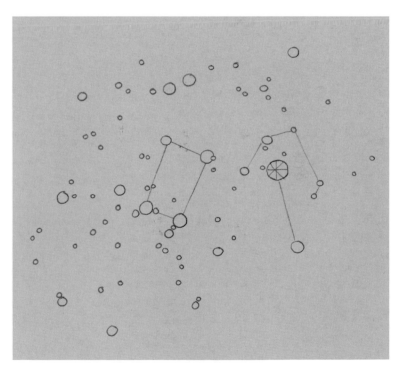

fig. 37   **The Mirror and Comb**
guiding star: Vega (Alpha Lyrae)

The brilliant blue-white star Vega is perceived as a great mirror next to a comb. Representing truth, self-knowledge and illumination, the mirror of lights in the night sky reflects the earth below. Adjacent is the comb, used for both personal adornment, and as a tool for preparing fibres in spinning and weaving. The teeth of a comb can be read as depicting the rays of the sun or, alternatively, as falling rain, and therefore as a potent symbol of fertility. Rectangular bone combs have been found in the Orkney and Shetland islands dating from the time of the Norse settlers, while in the iron-age beautiful mirrors were fashioned by the Celts from polished bronze. There are mirror-like shapes to be discerned in architectural remains; henges around stone circles, the large neolithic hall at Stanydale in Shetland, the bag-shaped building at Portmahomack. The Babylonians saw the mirror star as their messenger of light.

fig. 38   **The Boar on schist at Dunadd**

This fine pig, sus scrofa, is found far from the Pictish lands on north and east coasts, carved on an outcrop of dalradian rocks at Dunadd hillfort in the Kilmartin Glen, Argyll, a rocky stronghold, in use since the iron-age, surrounded by Mòine Mhòr, the great moss. On the same living rock, scoured by glaciers, a footprint is carved. This is the spot, the Albain Dalriada, where Fergus Mor, son of Erc, became first king. From the sixth to the ninth century the kings of Dalriada were inaugurated here, facing north, with a foot placed in the carved hollow. During this time, Dunadd was a major metalworking community, where skilled craft workers developed the insular style, and trade was done with peoples from as far south as the Mediteranean. On the east coast, the old name for St Andrews, centre of the early Pictish christians, was Muckross, the point of pigs. An area here still bears the name Boarhills. The wild boar is courageous, especially when defending her young. This admirable quality has led warriors, from ancient times until the present day, to choose the animal as their symbol and mascot. In Norse beliefs the gods Freyr and Freya each had boars with magical properties. The boar leads the animals of summer on the southern horizon. Zubeneschamali, the green star, is found on the boar's back.

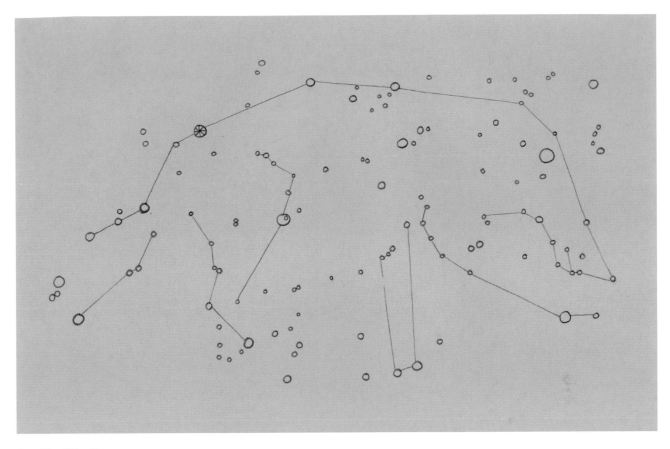

fig. 39 **The Boar**
guiding star: Zubeneschamali (Beta Librae)

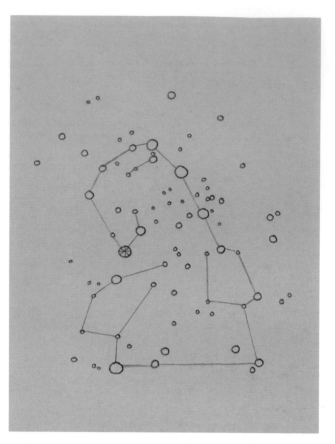

fig. 40 **The Water Horse on whinstone at Rhynie**

fig. 41 **The Water Horse**
guiding star: Antares (Alpha Scorpii)

There is a symbol that is rather horse-like, although we are only shown the head and upper body, and in place of legs it appears to have fins. This is the creature on a stone at Rhynie that I shall call the Water Horse. It is reminiscent of stories about the kelpie, a creature of water who could at times run over the land in the shape of a real horse, luring the unwitting into its watery home. The kelpie can be seen in the waves whipped up by the wind, dancing across the surface of lochs and streams.

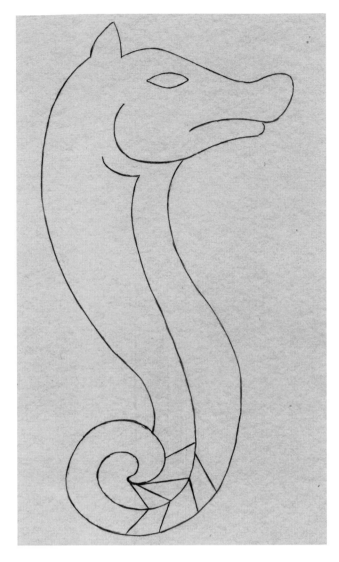

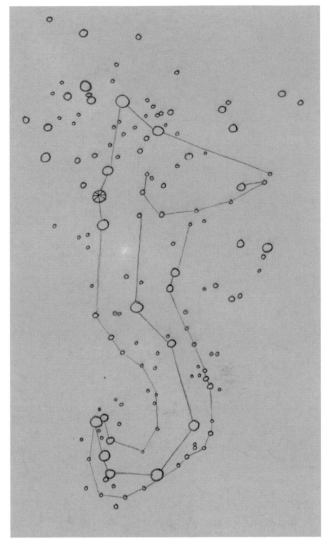

fig. 42   **The Seahorse on sandstone from Ulbster**

fig. 43   **The Seahorse**
guiding star: Antares (Alpha Scorpii)

Here is a late arrival, only found on stones of the early Christian era. Only the head of the seahorse can be observed from the Pictish lands, just above the horizon at mid-summer. Twinned seahorses were to play an important role in the imagery of later cross-slabs, seming to act as protective beings.

fig. 44   **The Horse on red granite at Inverurie**

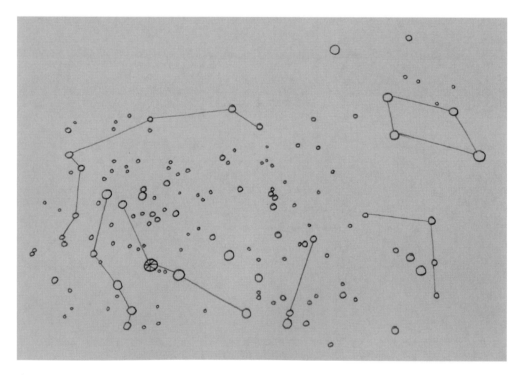

fig. 45   **The Horse**
  guiding star: Nunki (Sigma Sagittarii)

The star horse walks calmly through the milky way, a place of bright star clouds interspersed with dust clouds of light-absorbing dark matter. Eriskay ponies, native to the Western Isles, appear to be the survivors of those ridden by the Picts, their survival thanks to the remoteness of the isles. There are now only around three hundred left. These sturdy little horses have the long, thick-haired manes and tails from which the Picts spun the strings for their harps. In Buddhist symbolism, the horse can represent the hidden, indestructable nature of things; the Windhorse - Lung-ta - carries prayers on the winds. Given the horse's importance in the lives of the historical Picts, it is interesting that it is apparently rare among the early symbols.

fig. 46 **The Long-necked Bird**
guiding star: Altair (Alpha Aquilae)

A simple carving on the wall of Court Cave at Weymss of a long-necked goose or swan follows the lines of this star group. At present, however, it is not known to occur as a symbol on the Pictish stones.

AUTUMN STARS

f

ig. 47   **The Shield on sandstone from Golspie**

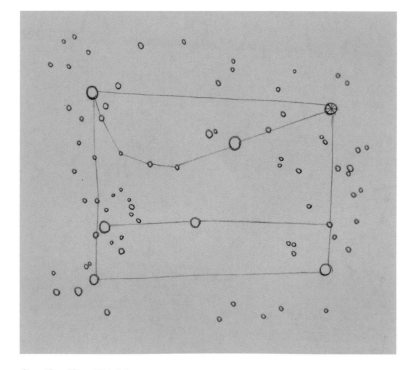

fig. 48   **The Shield**
guiding star: Almach (Gamma Andromedae)

The shield has the power to protect. On the Brough of Birsay stone from the Orkneys, three figures carry square shields. Figures of travelling monks, on the pictorial panels of the mighty stone crosses, carry rectangular bags slung around their necks, protection for the precious books of their new religion. The shield is a simple geometric shape, and as such shares in the wealth of symbolic meaning attached to rectangular forms, the compass rose, the four winds, the divisions of the year.

fig. 49   Two shields, very eroded, from the east wall of the Sloping Cave at East Weymss.

fig. 50　**The Doorway on sandstone at Aberlemno**

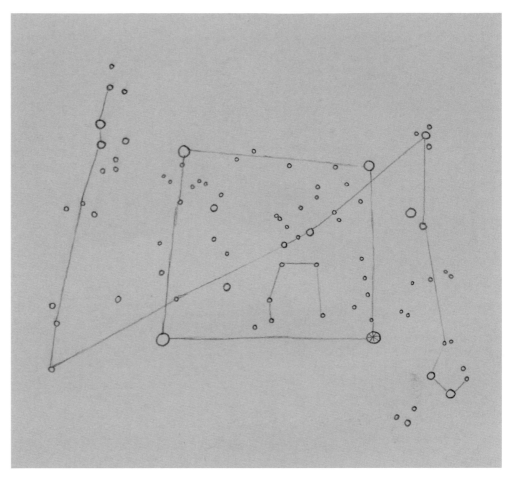

fig. 51 **The Doorway**
guiding star: Markab (Alpha Pegasi)

The doorway represents the threshhold of another realm. It can be seen as a literal representation of the doorway into a chamber tomb. It can also hold a spiritual meaning of communication between one world and another - passage between the living and the dead.

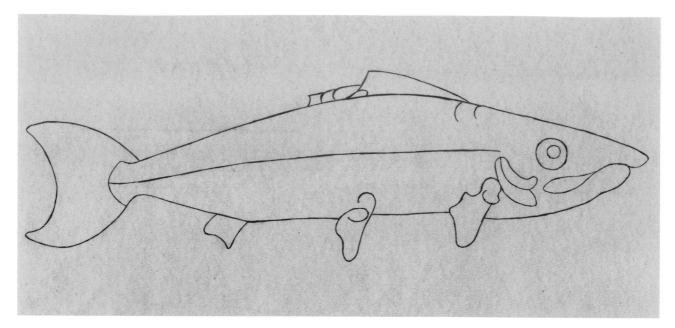

fig. 52 **The Salmon on red sandstone at Dunrobin**

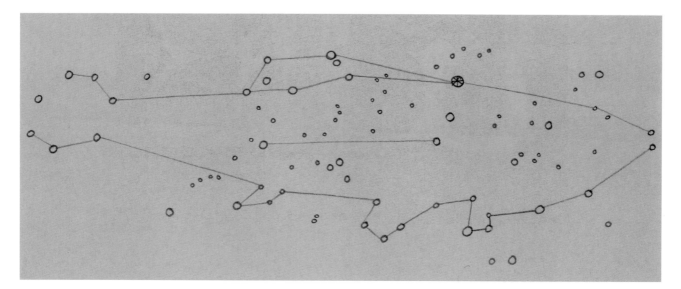

fig. 53 **The Salmon**
guiding star: Sadalsuud (Beta Aquarii)

The Atlantic salmon, salmo salar, use memories of star patterns as well as magnetic fields and minute chemical traces in the water of estuaries to return in winter to their river source of birth. The ability to survive in water both fresh and salt and the sheer determination demonstrated in leaping up-stream over rocks and torrents, were observed with wonder and admiration. Wisdom, fore-telling, knowledge from beyond this known world, are the qualities attributed to the salmon. She is often associated with sacred wells, a gleaming presence in the dark water. Traces of meaning survive in the stories of St Mungo/Kentigern and his finding of the ring in the fish. The salmon has feminine associations. In Egypt she is emblem of Isis and Hathor, while in Scandinavia an attribute of Frigga, standing for love and fertility.

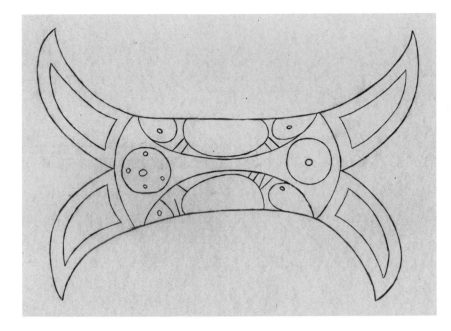

fig. 54　**The Double Crescent on pink sandstone at Dunrobin**

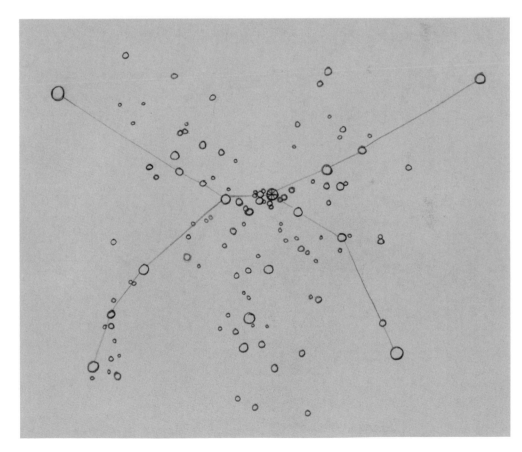

fig. 55　**The Double Crescent**
　　　　　guiding star: Algenib (Alpha Persei)

As Autumn draws on, the double crescent can be seen in the eastern sky and be compared to the crescent in the west. It rises overhead as the year progresses into winter. Two pairs of horns are tied together in this design. Ice haloes glowing with spectral colours can, on rare occasions, be seen high in the sky in this form. The Celts used the crescent moon and a design of two crescents back to back to symbolise immortality.

53

CIRCUMPOLAR STARS

FACING NORTH JULY

FACING NORTH NOVEMBER

FACING NORTH MARCH

fig. 56   Complex interlinking of the polar designs.

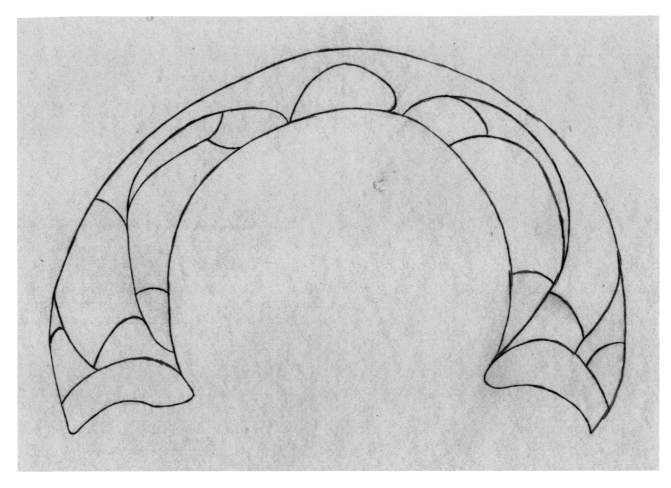

fig. 57 **The Arch on sandstone from Clynemilton**

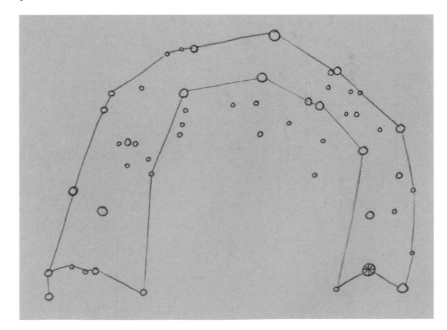

fig. 58 **The Arch**
guiding star: Polaris (Alpha Ursa Minoris)

This design may represent an arch or curved roof of some kind, thus symbolising shelter. Perhaps it is a connecting bridge, a pathway amongst the stars. At one end Polaris can be found, or, as the Celts knew it, An Gaelin; the beam that lights the way home. In the Viking age a bridge called Bifrost which gave access to Asgard, was guarded against the giants. This was said to be a rainbow linking heaven and earth, perhaps originally having been a representation of the milky way.

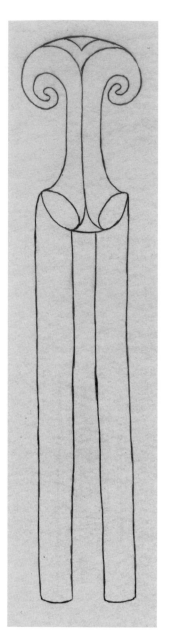

fig. 59   **The Pillars on red sandstone at Dunrobin**

fig. 60   **The Pillars**
         guiding stars: Polaris (Alpha Ursa Minoris)
         and Kochab (Beta Ursa Minoris)

The double pillars represent natural dualities, complementary opposites forming a balanced whole. The twin pillars rotate around the north celestial pole, the unmoving centre point of the turning heavens. The stars Polaris and Kochab are the terminals of the pillars extending from the right branch of the crescent. The early Egyptians, like other ancient people, believed that the earth rested and revolved upon one or more pillars. Since the pole star appears to be the only fixed point in the sky, they believed that the pillars of heaven were below this, and consequently were in the extreme north. The god of these world pillars was known to the Egyptians as Tat, to the Greeks as Atlas and to the Germanic peoples as Irmin. The Egyptians wrote of the north sea people, 'they come from the pillars of heaven'. Pillar symbolism exists in all the major religions; notably the two massive bronze pillars of Solomon's temple which formed the basis of masonic symbolism, and which are thought to have been represented amongst the pillars of Roslyn chapel near Edinburgh.

fig. 61   Design on a stone found in a burial deposit at
Gurness Broch, on Mainland, in the Orkneys
it seems to combine elements of the pillars,
doorway and well symbols.

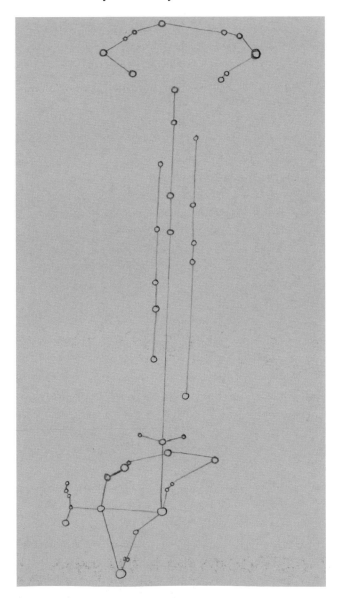

fig. 62   Plan of the Calanais standing stones, on Lewis,
in the Outer Hebrides. (These stones, however,
are rumoured to move around when
unobserved!)

fig. 63   Alignment of the pillars with the crescent and
V-branch.

fig. 64   **The Northfire on sandstone from Dunnichen**

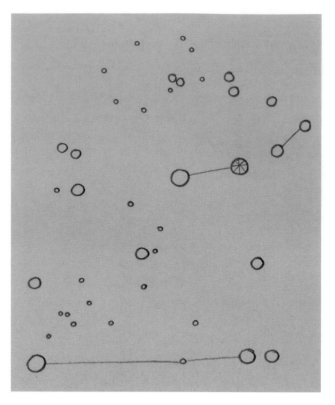

fig. 65   **The Northfire**
guiding star: Kochab (Beta Ursa Minoris)

The fire symbol is the spark of life. Light and heat are the complementary poles of fire. It is the volcanic formation of the land itself, symbol of the mountain and volcanic deities. It is the aurora borealis, dancing its fantastic dance across the sky. It is a symbol of purification and renewal of life. Companion of the metal smith, fire is essential for the art of transformation. An examination of surviving Pictish metalwork hints at an astonishing group of skilled workers producing weaponry, jewellery and precious ecclesiatical objects. Wild-silver wrought fluid into binding knots. In some cultures fire is represented by the mustard seed or the fir. Fire is wood transformed; the sources of wood, the trees, were regarded with reverence. The plant-like form of this symbol reflects this origin. On Scandinavian rock carvings an almost identical symbol is used to represent the smith's fire.

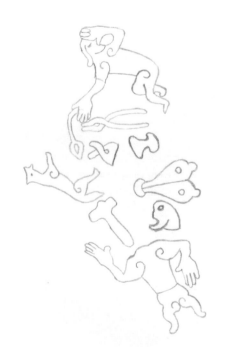

fig. 66   The Ramsund Rock, in Sodermanland, Sweden, depicts the myth of Sigurd, killer of Fafni the dragon. A fire symbol is placed with the tools of Regin the blacksmith.

60

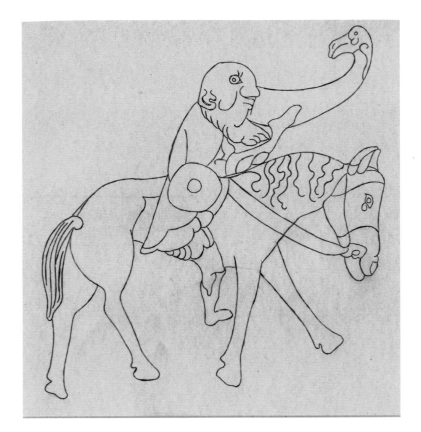

fig. 67   **The Rider on red sandstone from Invergowrie**

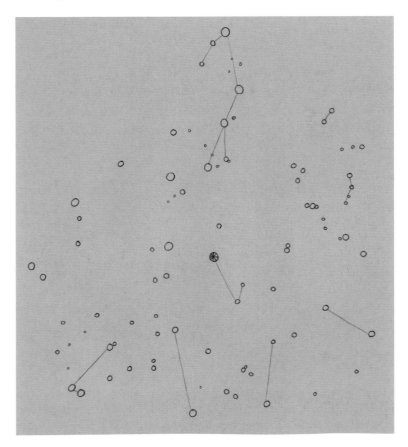

fig. 68   **The Rider**
            guiding star: Dubhe
            (Alpha Ursa Majoris)

He drinks from the bird-headed drinking horn which contains the waters of immortality; the rider is absorbing divine life and power. He has lived long; age bringing the wisdom gained with experience. His pony is aged too; plodding on, eternally circling the north pole. The aged man and pony both remind us of our own mortality. A parallel with the rider might be the Greek Silenus.

61

fig. 69   **The Serpent on whinstone at Brandsbutt**

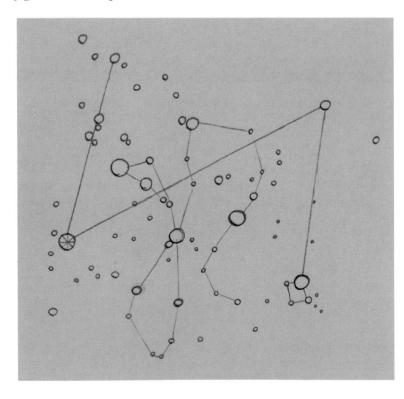

fig. 70   **The Serpent**
guiding star: Caph
(Beta Cassiopeiae)

The lightning serpent, thick and twisting, symbol of life energy. The serpent represents life and healing as it sheds its skin to reveal itself fresh and seemingly rejuvenated. The river Forth at Stirling is a good example of a river twisting and winding in the form of a great serpent. The Celtic serpent or dragon called Beithir was thought to live at the bottom of deep lochs. It was also regarded as a forest guardian dwelling in the deep waters found below the roots of trees. Throughout the world the serpent finds a place in myth and symbolism; sometimes in a benign role as healer or guardian; at other times taking on aspects of chaotic forces or of evil. The Babylonian dark serpent was Tiamat; in Norse tradition a great serpent gnawed ceaselessly at the roots of the world tree Yggdrasil; while in Tibet the guardian serpent is called Naga.

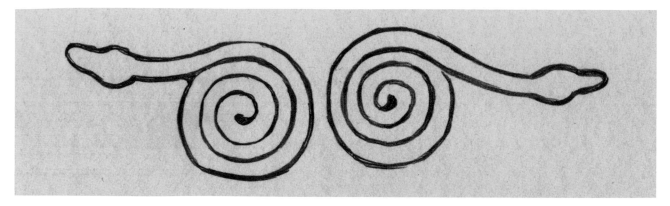

fig. 71 Carving of two serpents on a whinstone, now built into a garden wall at Kinnell Manse, Angus.

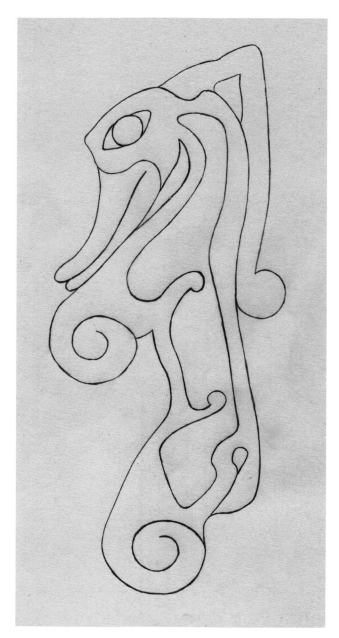

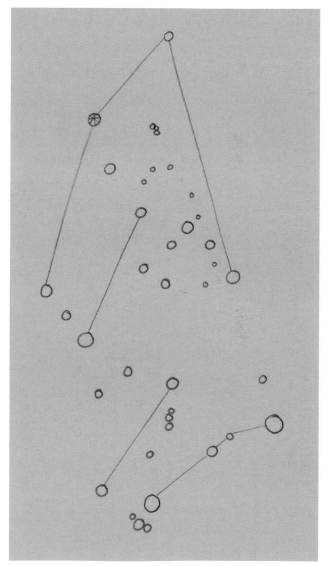

fig. 73 **The Upright Beastie**
guiding star: Errai (Gamma Cephei)

fig. 72 **The Upright Beastie on sandstone at Meigle**

The polar star beastie is a more compact reflection of the great winter star beastie. These have been described variously as swimming elephants, as dolphins and as dragons. Perhaps dragon is the closest; an imagined mythical being rather than a strangely mutated version of a real animal. Here we see the left flank of this crypto-zoological creature looking towards the serpent stars. During autumn and winter this beastie does a somersault, passing above Polaris.

Meanings

A very distinctive form of building is found in the Northern and Western Isles and throughout mainland Scotland. These are called brochs. They are thought to have been built from around the 5th to the 1st century BCE; although, as with other stone constructions, dating is very imprecise. Brochs are circular drystane towers with hollow walls containing narrow passages and stairways. They can be as high as forty feet or more. They have no exterior windows, however there are openings from the passages overlooking the interior space. They are shaped rather like cooling towers, tapering in towards the top. In the historical Pictish era some of the brochs in the Northern Isles, most notably the Broch of Gurness, were partly demolished and the stones used to build houses. Up until recent times, the more complete brochs were used as dwellings but there are no signs that this was their original purpose. If we are to accept the theory that they were defensive structures, evidence that they have ever been attacked is not apparent.

Associated Pictish artifacts are the enigmatic painted beach pebbles found around broch sites. The earliest, from Scatness in Shetland, date from around 100BCE. Simple designs of dots, circles, crescents and wavy lines have been applied to naturally rounded quartzite pebbles using lampblack.

The brochs are similar in form and structure to the nuraghi of Sardinia. The nuraghi were written about by the Greek author Timaeus in about 300 BCE and they were old even then as he attributes their constuction to the legendary craftsman Daedalus - also said to have been responsible for building the labyrinth for Minos. Radiocarbon testing has now dated these structures to somewhere between 1400 and 1200 BCE. Their name is possibly derived from the Phoenician word nur-hag meaning tower of fire and they are thought to have been sun temples, used in rituals connected with solar and lunar eclipses. Could our brochs have been used for rituals and measurements connected with astronomical events? I feel that this is highly likely. There had been a great deal of historical precedent for ritual observatories in the form of the stone circles. Calanais on the island of Lewis is site of perhaps the finest megalithic lunar observatory. Given the importance of the stars to the Picts, it is perfectly plausible that they would have had special places for their study. It is more comfortable to look at the stars lying down, especially those directly overhead. 'Up' and 'down' then depends on which direction your head lies. Imagine lying in the central chamber of a broch, looking up through the open top at the night stars framed in a circle.

fig. 74 Dún Chàrlabhaign Broch, Eilean Leòdhais.

The myths of the Norse people seem to have a close affinity with the symbols of the Picts. My own feeling is that the early people of Scotland (before the Scots lent that country their name) outlying on the edge of the northern sea, were more closely connected to the early Scandinavian people in their stories and beliefs than to the Celts in the south. In particular, the carved stones on the Baltic sea island of Gotland speak of communication across the cold waves of the north sea.

fig. 75   Sketches of imagery on the Gotland stones, erected between the 5th and the 12th
century. Many of the stones are now held in the Länsmuseet på Gotland. Others
are in the Historiska Museet, Stockholm.
A. Sanda; B. Austers at Hangvar; C. Martebo Parish Church; D. Ire in Hellvi;
E. Broa in Halla; F. Smiss at Närr; G. Smiss at Garda.

The complexity of meaning found in the symbols has, I believe, a very ancient heritage as a comparison with the designs painted on neolithic ceramics can show. Marija Gimbutas describes pots from around 4000 BCE found in eastern Europe. Guardian dogs are shown surrounding the life tree. There are deer transformed into whirling crescents, heads in the shape of crescent moons, comb-like shapes and winding snakes, opposed crescents and egg-like containers.

The Pictish symbols can be seen to have roots in the most ancient symbols used by northern people, and probably derive from the concepts of the earliest stone circle builders. The crescent tomb of the eagles was built in 3120 BCE which may make it a lot older than the circles. The Double Disc has a long lineage, developing from the Palaeolithic double-egg of about 6000 BCE. This represents the creation story. Egyptian, Babylonian, Hindu and Greek mythologies all preserve these myths of the universe as a cosmic egg from which deities emerge and which was created by a cosmic snake or bird from the primeval waters. In Egypt the egg was laid by the Nile goose, creator of the world. Then the egg split in two! The cosmic egg becomes the double spiral of the Hanubut world pillar Irminsul, the volute of the Greek pillar, the French fleur-de-lys. It is the symbol for North and this is exactly what we have on the floriated V-branches and Z-branches found joined with certain symbols of the Picts. The pole star appears to remain fixed in the night sky, while the entire field of stars revolves around it. A carving on a stone is fixed on the earth. At certain times of the night, at certain times of the year, particular stars will align with angles of the V and Z branches. Where we can be certain that a stone remains situated in its original site, it would be illuminating to record the stars on which these pointers align at different times of the year.

The symbols contain various qualities of the elements of life. There is water: humid, fluid and cohesive; air: dry, light and mobile; fire: hot, consuming and mobile; and earth: cold, solid and load-bearing. The elements of life interact with each other. So fire and earth are combined as metal in the work of the smith. Fire and water are the active and the passive; as such they are in conflict, but as heat and moisture they are necessary for all life. The serpent inhabits caves and hollows. The eagle soars towards the heavens. The Lightning Serpent is fire within water, the Sea Eagle fire over water. The fish - in particular the Salmon - and the serpent are, as representations of female and male genitals, symbolic of reproduction and fertility. The fish, however, has a deeper meaning as a vehicle of the soul, and it retains this meaning in Christian symbolism. The serpent - and its derivative the spiral, are among the earliest symbols used by humans. It is symbolic of nature's dynamism; the vehicle of immortality, and it is water, the primordial element, representing the earliest concept of the genesis of the universe from an elemental aqua-substance. To the Picts, as to their ancesters, the mysteries of life lay in water: oceans, lochs, rivers, wells and springs. Reflected in still water, visible in the night sky, they drew inspiration and imagined the symbols of life's mysteries.

A tiny number of of old writings give us clues to the history of the Picts. An extremely important document is held in the Bibliothèque Nationale, Paris. The Poppleton manuscript, Compiled in York, was written down sometime in the fourteenth century. It contains copies of seven Scottish documents the originals of which probably date to between 1202 and 1214, in the reign of William Rufus, better known as the Lion. One is known as 'De Situ Albanie'. It begins; 'De Situ Albanie que in se figuram hominis habet quomodo fuit primitus is septum regionibus diuisa quibusque nominibus antiquitus sit uocata et a quibus inhabitata'; In regard to Albania, shaped in the form of a man, how it was first divided into seven kingdoms, their ancient names and inhabitants. It then goes on to name the seven areas which are thought to have corresponded to the seven Pictish kingdoms. The other texts include a wonderfully imaginative 'Cronica de origine antiquorum Pictorum', an account of the foundation of Saint Andrews and lists of kings; a list of Pictish kings; a list of kings ruling over both Picts and Scots where the land is referred to as Pictavia; and a list of kings ruling over Alba, the name given by gaelic speakers to the land.

Over time, the power holders in the land changed, the languages changed, the names changed. The Roman invaders had called the land Caledonia, 'land of the Caledonii'. Later monastic scribes used Pictavia. While Alba would remain the gaelic name for the land, Scotia was used to describe present day Scotland from the middle ages onwards. It is found in the Chronicum Saxonium, a collection of writings placed in various monasteries throughout England. Derived from the Latin word scotia, it was first used to describe land inhabited by the gaelic-speaking Scotti. During the Scottish wars of independance, Ireland was called Scotia major, while Scotland was called Scotia Minor. A clear idea of the changes going on during the time of the Picts is very difficult to surmise. Not least because the available written documents were produced for, and designed to please, later ruling families and church leaders who likely had a preferred version of past events.

The coming of Christianity to the land of the Picts did not put an end to the carving of the Pictish star symbols. The designs were intermingled with scenes from the old testament on elaborate stone crosses. Whatever symbolic meaning these designs held, they could not have been at odds with the beliefs and teachings of these early Christians. The first Christian teachers brought with them a wealth of new learning from the Roman world, the Greek world, and further afield. This would have included knowledge of astronomy, including the work of the Greek astronomer and geographer Ptolemy. It would also have included knowledge of the mythological images used by the Babylonians and the Greeks to illustrate the constellations. The Christian bible contains references to certain stars and constellations. In the old testament these had been used to reflect on God's greatness as a powerful being with the ability to place the stars in the sky. In Amos the Lord is the maker of the seven stars and Orion. Job refers to the crooked serpent, Arcturus, Orion and the Pliedes. He is asked by God 'Canst thou bind the sweet influences of the Pliedes, or loose the bands of Orion?' In Saint Mathew's Gospel there is the account of the wise men and the star of the nativity. In the Acts of the Apostles Paul sails in an Alexandrian ship called the Castor and Pollux. The Pliedes appear within the symbolic imagery found in the Revelations of Saint John the Divine. The morning star had been used in the old testament as a symbol of the coming messiah and in the new testament it became a symbol of Christ.

Monasteries provided stability and refuge from the outside world. They were places of study where applied astronomy was practised. The movements of the stars were observed and used to calculate the hours of prayer. While the sun could be used as the clock for the daytime divisions, the stars were essential for the accurate regulation of the observances of the night. Just as the gardeners of the monasteries gathered knowledge about soil, plant growth and medicinal properties from long hours of work and observation, so the timekeepers looked to the stars and found the skies to be a fundamental source of learning. Calendar makers studied the luner and solar cycles and used their findings for the complicated task of determining the correct days for religious celebrations, in particular the dating of Easter. Accurate dating would also have been required for the interpretation of biblical prophecies.

Astronomy also played an important role in the planning and situating of religious buildings. In the Hebrides and the Northern Isles, as well as in Ireland, Monastic chapels built of drystane were placed so that their windows framed the rising sun on the feast day of an important saint - the most frequent being the feasts of Patrick on March 17th and Aidan on August 31st. Saint Patrick's day coincided with the Spring Equinox. At Saint Andrews a series of buildings were erected to house the relics of the saint. The cruciform church of St Mary on the Crag was built around the end of the eighth century; the church of St Rule, with its tower of grey sandstone ashler rising 108 feet high, was built around 1127; and work on St Andrew's Cathedral began in 1159. These buildings shared a common feature with other Christian architecture; an east-west orientation allowing worshippers to face east and the rising of the morning star.

The Pictish symbols as astronomical representations would have sat easily alongside the new Christian symbolism of the cross. A stone found in the foundations of the old kirk at Arbirlot in 1852 has an intriguing design of aligned crosses and rectangular forms, which may have been intended to represent books, carved on hard blue whinstone. It appears to be an early use of the cross on stone and there is known to have been an early Christian community in the area. The twin crosses on the stone are formed using the same geometry found in the crescent symbol. Perhaps on this stone the sculptor was experimenting with the combination of old and new symbolism. For a time the Pictish symbols were combined with the new Christian symbols in carvings of great complexity and beauty. At some point the use of the old symbols was discontinued. We do not know whether this was a sudden change or whether it happened gradually. It may have been a deliberate policy by a ruling class who wished to deny any connection with the Picts, or it may be that over time, latin learning, with the greco-roman systems of astrological practise, simply displaced the native systems, and the knowledge of the asterisms, which had given shape to the symbols, was lost.

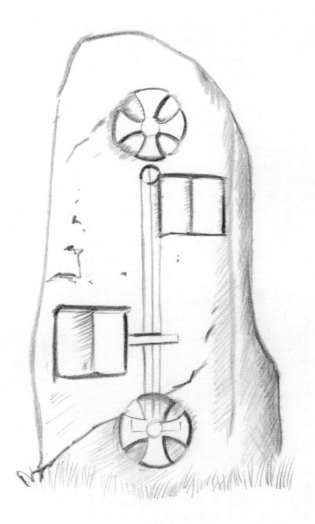

In 1986 a near-earth asteroid was discovered by Glasgow astronomer J. Duncan Waldron. Around five kilometers in diameter, this space body travels in an elliptic orbit around the sun. It shares the orbit of the earth and is sometimes called the earth's second moon. It was named Cruithne after the legendary first king of the Picts. Although the Pictish astronomers would not have observed this asteroid as it is never visible to the naked eye, I like to think they would have been pleased by this tribute.

List of Illustrations

Bibliography

For further reading on the Picts and their arts
CUMMINS, W. A., *The Age of the Picts,* Stroud: Sutton Publishing, 1998
GORDON, C. A., 'The Pictish Animals Observed', *Proceedings of the Society of Antiquaries of Scotland,* CXVIII, 1964-66, pp. 215-224, plates XXVII-XXXI
HENDERSON, G. and I. HENDERSON, *The Art of the Picts: Sculpture and Metalwork in Early Medieval Scotland,* London: Thames and Hudson Ltd., 2004
HENDERSON, I., '(i) Flemington Farm, Aberlemno, Angus', and A. SMALL, '(ii) Fairy Green, Collace, Perthshire with a note of a stone cup from the same farm', 'Two Pictish Symbol Stones', *P. S. A. S.,* XCV,1961-62, pp. 219-222, plate XIII
MACLAGAN, C., 'Notes on the Sculptured Caves near Dysart, in Fife, Illustrated by Drawings of the Sculptures', *P. S. A. S.,* XI, January 11, 1875, pp. 107-120, plates III-IV
MORRISON, Rev. J., 'Note on the Discovery of an Incised Symbol-bearing Slab at Easterton of Roseisle, Elginshire', *P. S. A. S.,* May 13, 1895 pp. 449-453
RANKIN. F, *Guide to Wemyss Caves,* East Weymss: Save Wemyss Ancient Caves Society, 2001
RITCHIE, A., 'Painted Pebbles in Early Scotland', P. S. A. S., 104, 1971-2, pp. 297-301, plate 42
RITCHIE, J. N. G., 'Two New Pictish Stones from Orkney', P. S. A. S., 101, 1968-69, pp. 130-133, plate 10
SHEPHERD, I. A. G. and A. N. SHEPHERD, 'An Incised Pictish Figure and a New Symbol Stone from Barflat, Rhynie, Gordon District', *P. S. A. S.,* 109, 1977-8, pp. 211-222, plates 11-12
SIMPSON, M., 'Massive Armlets in the North British Iron Age', *Studies in Ancient Europe: Essays presented to Stuart Piggott,* Leicester University Press, 1968, pp., 233-254, plates VI-X
WAINWRIGHT, F. T. (editor), *The Problem of the Picts: Studies in History and Archaeology,* Perth: Melven Press, 1980
WALKER, I. C., 'Easterton of Roseisle: a forgotten site in Moray', *Studies in Ancient Europe: Essays presented to Stuart Piggott,* Leicester University Press, 1968, pp., 95-115
YOUNG, H. W., 'The Ancient Bath at Burghead, with remarks on it's origins as shewn by existing baths of the same shape and design', *P. S. A. S.,* January 13, 1890, pp. 147-156; 'Notes on Further Excavations at Burghead', *P. S. A. S.,* February 13, 1893, pp. 86-91

There are many published guides to the night sky; this one has clear diagrams and photographs of the eighty-eight established constellations
SANFORD, J., *Observing the Constellations,* London: Guild Publishing, 1989

For deeper study and comparison of symbolic meaning; I recommend the following
COOPER, J. C., *An Illustrated Encyclopedia of Traditional Symbols,* London: Thames and Hudson, 1993
DAVIDSON, H. R. E., *Myths and Symbols in Pagan Europe: Early Scandinavian and Celtic Religions,* Manchester University Press, 1988
GIMBUTAS, M., *The Goddesses and Gods of Old Europe 6500-3500BC: Myths and Cult Images,* London: Thames and Hudson, 1982
MACKENZIE, Rev. J. B., 'Notice of Two Stone Axes, One Ornamented with an Incised Interlaced Pattern, Found at Balnahannait, Loch Tay', *P. S. A. S.,* May 18, 1901, pp. 310-313
MACKILLOP, J., *Dictionary of Celtic Mythology,* Oxford University Press, 1998
MACMILLAN, Rev. H., 'Notice of Two Boulders having rain-filled cavities on the shores of Loch Tay, formerly associated with the cure of disease', *P. S. A. S.,* June 9, 1884, pp.m 369-376
MCNEILL, F. M., *The Silver Bough, Volume one: Scottish Folk-Lore and Folk Belief,* Edinburgh: Canongate Classics, 2001
MEGAW, J. V. S. (editor), *To illustrate the monuments: Essays on archaeology presented to Stuart Piggott,* London, Thames and Hudson, 1976
SMITH, B., 'Isbister, an Orkney Islands Council Guardianship Monument', *P. S. A. S.,* 119, 1989, pp. 55-58

Websites
University of Strathclyde, Pictish Stones Search Facility: **www.stams.strath.ac.uk/research/pictish/database.php**
Save Wemyss Ancient Caves Society: **www.wemysscaves.co.uk**
Proceedings of the Society of Antiquaries of Scotland: **http://onlinebooks.library.upenn.edu/webbin/serial?id=prosascot**
Isbister Chambered Cairn: **www.tomboftheeagles.co.uk**
Scottish Rocks: **www.scottishgeology.com**
Native Scottish Woodland, a Forestry Commission booklet: **www.forestry.gov.uk/pdf/nws.pdf/$FILE/nws.pdf**

Locations of the stones carved with the designs which inspired the illustrations in this book

Aberlemno 2: The Doorway
Aberlemno Kirkyard, Angus

Ardross 2: The Red Deer
Clynemilton 1: The Arch
Inverness Museum, Castle Wynd, Inverness

Brandsbutt: The Serpent
Brandsbutt Housing Estate, Inverurie, Aberdeenshire

Brodie/Rodney's Stone: The Star Animal, The Stars in the Well
In the grounds of; Brodie Castle, near Forres, Moray

Bullion/Invergowrie 2: The Rider
Burghead 1: The Bull
Easterton of Roseisle: The Goose
Grantown: The Stag
Hilton of Cadboll: The Crescent
Museum of Scotland, Chambers Street, Edinburgh

Dunadd: The Boar
Near the Crinan Canal at; Dunadd Hillfort, Kilmartin Glen, Argyll and Bute

Dunnichen: The Double Disc, The Mirror and Comb, The Northfire
The Meffan Museum and Art Gallery, 20 West High Street, Forfar, Angus

Dunrobin 1: The Salmon, The Pillars
Dunrobin 2: The Double Crescent
Golspie/Craigton 2: The Winter Giant, The Shield
Dunrobin Castle Museum, Golspie, Sutherland

Gurness: The Bear
In the care of; Shetland Amenity Trust, Garthpool, Lerwick, Shetland

Inverurie: The Horse
Inverurie Cemetery, Aberdeenshire

Meigle 5: The Well, The Upright Animal
Meigle Sculptured Stone Museum, Dundee Road, Meigle, Perthshire

Newbiggen, Leslie: The Wolf
In the gardens of; Leith Hall, Leslie, south of Huntly, Aberdeenshire

Rhynie 5: The Water Horse
Just outside the gates of; The Old Kirkyard, Rhynie, south of Huntly, Aberdeenshire

Rhynie 7: The Summer Giant:
In the council building; Woodhill House, Westburn Road, Aberdeen

Strathpeffer/Clach an Tiompain: The Eagle
On a hillside to the east of; Strathpeffer, near Dingwall, Ross and Cromarty

Ulbster: The Seahorse
Thurso Museum, Caithness

Artist/Designer Heather Connie Martin
was born in Dundee in 1962.
During the 1980s she studied design at Dundee and
Glasgow. Early and abiding influences in her work are:
a love of colour, fascination with the remains of the past,
the patterns of the stars, the language of rocks.
She lived for twenty years in Glasgow, selling books in
the time-honoured tradition from a street barrow.
She now works from her attic studio under the chestnut
beams and rough slate tiles of an old house in
the southern Cevennes in France. Moving from the gritty
urban spaces of Glasgow to the peace of the mountains;
walking the hard schist paths over the ridges; experienc-
ing the divisions of the seasons in a place of hot mediter-
ranean summers, dramatic thunderstorms and icy white
winters.
Drawing on her years of study of Pictish and Celtic
culture; she creates paintings and woven panels full of
symbolic imagery in rich earth colours.